baches & cribs

a pictorial journey through New Zealand's favourite holiday places

baches & cribs

a pictorial journey through New Zealand's favourite holiday places

Jeff Grigor

PENGUIN BOOKS

PENGUIN BOOKS

Published by the Penguin Group

Penguin Group (NZ), 67 Apollo Drive, Rosedale,
North Shore 0632, New Zealand (a division of Pearson New Zealand Ltd)
Penguin Group (USA) Inc., 375 Hudson Street,
New York, New York 10014, USA
Penguin Group (Canada), 90 Eglinton Avenue East, Suite 700, Toronto,
Ontario, M4P 2Y3, Canada (a division of Pearson Penguin Canada Inc.)
Penguin Books Ltd, 80 Strand, London, WC2R 0RL, England
Penguin Ireland, 25 St Stephen's Green,
Dublin 2, Ireland (a division of Penguin Books Ltd)
Penguin Group (Australia), 250 Camberwell Road, Camberwell,
Victoria 3124, Australia (a division of Pearson Australia Group Pty Ltd)
Penguin Books India Pvt Ltd, 11, Community Centre,
Panchsheel Park, New Delhi - 110 017, India
Penguin Books (South Africa) (Pty) Ltd, 24 Sturdee Avenue,
Rosebank, Johannesburg 2196, South Africa

Penguin Books Ltd, Registered Offices: 80 Strand, London, WC2R 0RL, England

First published by Penguin Group (NZ), 2008
1 3 5 7 9 10 8 6 4 2

Copyright © Jeff Grigor, 2008

The right of Jeff Grigor to be identified as the author of this work in terms of
section 96 of the Copyright Act 1994 is hereby asserted.

Designed and typeset by Pindar (NZ)
Printed in Hong Kong through Bookbuilders

ISBN 978 014300923 8
A catalogue record for this book is available
from the National Library of New Zealand.

www.penguin.co.nz

INTRODUCTION

Bach is a unique New Zealand word. Its definition in the *Reed Dictionary of New Zealand English* is 'a weekend or beach cottage'. But in Otago and Southland these are known as cribs, and for some strange reason in South Canterbury they are commonly referred to as huts.

The first baches were built early last century at beaches, lakes and rivers that were close to towns and cities, but as roads and transportation improved they were built in more remote areas – mostly where there was water for fishing or swimming. The golden age for bach building was the two decades after World War Two. They were often built (without a building permit) on land that may have been donated by a generous farmer; on Crown land without permission; on Maori land at a peppercorn rental; and in many cases close to water on the Queen's Chain. Many bach owners held no legal title for the land they built on.

Baches have become part of the fabric of our lives – an icon of Kiwiana. But today, they look increasingly vulnerable and I fear, due to a number of pressures, that many are destined to disappear in the near future.

Those built on Crown land or the Queen's Chain are threatened by the Department of Conservation with destruction or removal, and many of the baches in this book may be no more within the next few years, or when their current owners are deceased. Areas affected by these disputes include Rangitoto Island, the Nelson Boulder Bank, Taylors Mistake in Christchurch and Lake Alexandrina in the Mackenzie Basin. District and regional councils now legally require sewerage and drainage facilities that were unimaginable when the baches were built, and this threatens other settlements.

But the greatest threat to the New Zealand bach is the spiralling demand for land by water or with a view of it, which has led to the land that the bach is typically built on being worth many times what the bach alone is worth. Consequently, at holiday settlements all over New Zealand humble baches are being torn down and replaced with architecturally designed mansions, which are often too large for the site and out of keeping with their surroundings.

I count myself as being very fortunate that in the mid 1950s my parents bought a hut in the Waipopo settlement on the banks of the Opihi River about two kilometres from the river mouth. The hut (as can be seen in the following photo) was basic. A bunkroom for us boys, an enclosed porch with a three-quarter bed for my parents, and a kitchen/ living room. Water was obtained from a well with a hand pump that had to be primed before use, and the water carried into the house in kerosene tins – a daily chore for me and my brother. The toilet was a long drop dug by hand that was situated as far as possible from the hut. The one concession to modern living was electricity, but of course there was no telephone and television had yet to be introduced to New Zealand. All bathing was done in the river, which was clean and warm.

We loved it. As soon as school holidays commenced, the family packed up and moved to Waipopo for the summer's duration. When he was not on holiday, my father would commute daily the twenty kilometres into Timaru to work. For my brothers and me life was one great long holiday. We had our own canoe and we roamed the eight kilometres of river between the State Highway 1 bridge and the river mouth with a freedom unknown to the children of today. We often took our own lunch and cooked sausages over a fire by the river. Life jackets were unheard of. We swam and fished for trout (illegally with gaffs and spears) in the Opihi River and for flounder in the lagoons by the river mouth. At night we fished by torch light with spear, gaff and rotten meat for eels, which could measure up to five feet in length.

My wife Rose's family had baches at Charteris Bay on Banks Peninsula and they had similar summer holidays, with an emphasis on boating and water sports. They also spent all their summer holiday at the bach, and often shifted out there before school finished. Rose has fond memories of catching the launch from Diamond Harbour to Lyttelton and the train to Christchurch to attend school.

We have also been very fortunate to be invited by friends to holiday with them at some of the wonderful baches that are featured in this book. Some of the most memorable holidays of our married life have been spent in baches at Lake Alexandrina, in a mountain cottage at over 5000 feet in the Southern Alps, at Purakaunui on the Otago Peninsula, on Scroggs Hill high above Brighton Beach south of Dunedin, at Buckletons Bay east of Warkworth and in Queenstown.

The reason for compiling this book was to produce a permanent record of some of the more unusual and iconic baches still remaining in New Zealand, and we are extremely grateful to all those who sent us photos. We hoped that by inviting people throughout New Zealand to contribute their photos we would be rewarded with outstanding portraits of iconic and interesting baches and we have not been disappointed.

Our family hut at Waipopo, South Canterbury.
Alma Grigor

NORTH ISLAND

Rangitoto Island.
Susan Geck

Northland, east of
Paihia. This bach was
built in the early 1970s
in a secluded part of the
Whangaruru Harbour,
near Bland Bay. It fronts
onto a private, sandy
beach and is enjoyed
every year by three
generations of the
original owner's family.
*Photo provided by
Sarah Ayton*

Matapouri, a short distance north of Tutukaka, is a part of New Zealand where seaside property prices have skyrocketed. I was therefore delighted to see that there are still Kiwi baches in prime positions in this area.
Carole Emanuel

LEFT, RIGHT AND FOLLOWING PAGE

These six baches are situated in the Sandspit Motor Camp, east of Warkworth. They all have different names: Corporate Box, Shoe Box, Match Box, Chocolate Box and Udder Box.

David Heap

The baches on Rangitoto Island, like a number in New Zealand, are under threat from the Department of Conservation. I am bemused by the fact that a department tasked with the job of conserving our heritage is so keen to destroy these examples of our history.
Derek Miles

LEFT
Rangitoto Island.
Doug Humby

RIGHT AND BELOW
Rangitoto Island.
Doug Humby

LEFT
Rangitoto Island.
Jim Harding

LEFT
Rangitoto Island.

RIGHT
Waiheke Island has a reputation for being a holiday resort for Auckland's rich and famous – these photos disprove that. The New Zealand bach is alive and well on Waiheke. This houseboat, on the Ostend Estuary, is a perfect example.

BOTTOM RIGHT
Something completely different on Waiheke Island, off Shelly Beach Road.

BOTTOM FAR RIGHT
Definitely original at Blackpool Beach, Waiheke Island.
Doug Humby

LEFT
Houseboats in the mangroves, Putiki Estuary, Waiheke Island.

RIGHT
Backup accommodation in the caravan at Rocky Bay, Waiheke Island.

FAR RIGHT
A weekender, Ostend Estuary, Waiheke Island.

BOTTOM
No stress living, Waiheke Island.
Doug Humby

ABOVE
Ostend Road, Waiheke Island.

RIGHT
A work in progress, Omiha, Waiheke Island.
Doug Humby

Ostend Estuary boathouse. *Tsunami* is twenty years old and was originally used to transport animals from Auckland to Waiheke Island. Kiran, the current owner, is pictured on board.
Doug Humby

LEFT
Bruce and Nellie Shaw purchased the section for £995 and the bach remains in family ownership. Could you imagine selling a site that enjoys this view?

RIGHT
Situated on Captain Cook Road, Cooks Beach, Coromandel Peninsula. The bach was built in 1965 by the Taplin brothers at a cost of £1200. The materials were transported over a tortuous gravel road from Hamilton.

Tracey Shaw

Waihi Beach, Bay of Plenty.
Beverly Holland

LEFT
Pencarrow (named after Nelle Scanlon's book) was built in 1934 by Beverly Holland's father and uncle. It has been extended and altered since then.

BOTTOM
Pencarrow, Waihi Beach.
Beverly Holland

BACHES & CRIBS

THIS PAGE AND RIGHT
Whitebaiters' baches, Port Waikato.
I love the water supply arrangements.
Susan Geck

Grounded UFO, Raglan.
Sarah Biss

Baches at Mokau, north of New Plymouth.
Joan Titchener

Hawke's Bay is endowed with many excellent beaches and has a rich collection of genuine Kiwi baches. The following are splendid examples.

LEFT
Haumoana, east of Hastings.

BELOW
Cliffs' beach house, Grange Road, Haumoana.
This small house designed by the eminent architect J. W. Chapman-Taylor in 1921 started out as a small bach for the Cliffs, a well-known Hastings family.
It is now a two-storey cottage of reinforced concrete construction. Due to the sunken nature of the entry level, the house could easily be mistaken for a single-storey cottage.
Alwyn Corban

Settlement at Ocean Beach, south of Havelock North.
Alwyn Corban

Ocean Beach,
Hawke's Bay.
Alwyn Corban

THIS PAGE AND RIGHT
Pourerere, east of Waipukurau.
Alwyn Corban

Waipatiki, Hawke's Bay.
Alwyn Corban

Te Awanga, east of Hastings.
Alwyn Corban

LEFT

This bach, sitting five metres from the sand at Castle Point, east of Masterton, is still substantially the same as it was when built in the 1940s. High tides and easterly storms straight off the Pacific Ocean occasionally send waves flowing under the house. However, the solid totara piles and the sea walls have kept the ocean from destroying it thus far.
David Hedley

RIGHT

This corrugated iron beauty is situated at Herbertville, Wairarapa.
Susan Geck

LEFT

Near Ngawi on the road
to Cape Palliser, the
southernmost point of
the North Island.
Sarah Biss

THIS PAGE AND NEXT
An eclectic group of
baches at Makara Beach,
west of Wellington City.
David Emanuel

Houghton Bay, between Lyall Bay and Island Bay, faces directly south to Cook Strait.
David Emanuel

SOUTH ISLAND

LEFT
This bach at Bark Bay in the Abel Tasman National Park was built in 1957 by Rollo Wilkinson, Kelvin Wilkinson and builder, C. D. Grieve.

Famous guests who have stayed here include Dame Cath Tizard and American Ambassador Charles J. Swindell, who both sent commemorative plaques that are displayed above the bach's fireplace.
Pamela Phillips

PREVIOUS PAGE
Bark Bay in the Abel Tasman Park.

In England, these are referred to as 'follies'. A bach designed to resemble a lighthouse, complete with jetty, rowboat and artificial seagulls. Ligar Bay, Golden Bay.

John Barton

TOP AND LEFT
On the beach at Marahau, the southern boundary of the Abel Tasman National Park.
John Barton

RIGHT
This is an original musterer's hut which was rebuilt in 1929. Graham Valley, Motueka.
Rebecca Bowater

At first glance it looks like the Middle East, but it is in fact the Nelson Boulder Bank, a natural breakwater that protects Nelson Harbour. There are a number of baches on it. None have electricity and are accessible only by boat.
Barry Doig

Looking out across the harbour to Nelson City.
Rebecca Bowater

LEFT AND RIGHT
No shortage of driftwood.
Barry Doig

It gets very hot on the boulders during a Nelson summer, and owners say that at night they can hear them moving.
Rebecca Bowater

TOP
Rebecca Bowater

BOTTOM
Port Nelson is straight across the water.
Barry Doig

RIGHT
Mahau Sound, Marlborough Sounds.
Jan Borland

LEFT
Raetihi, Double Bay, Marlborough Sounds.
Geoff Cloake

RIGHT
This charming old bach, off Queen Charlotte Sound, is accessible only by boat.
Rose Grigor

BOTTOM
The bach enjoys a wonderful view down Lochmara Bay.
Rose Grigor

Woodpecker Bay, ten kilometres north of Punakaiki on the West Coast. The McMillan family has owned this bach for thirty years. The inside is cosy and closely resembles the interior of many other baches throughout New Zealand.
Craig McMillan

Fox River, southern end of Woodpecker Bay. The Department of Conservation has a draft rule that says all baches on their West Coast land should go by 2025.
Jo Edgar

FAR LEFT AND ABOVE
Fox River.

LEFT
This old coal miner's
cottage in Blackball has
been preserved as a
charming holiday bach.
Jo Edgar

Otira, Westland.
An old roadman's
cottage dating
back to the
beginning of
the twentieth
century.
Rochelle Rafferty

LEFT

Cascade River below Jackson Bay, South Westland. Maurice 'The Bull' Nolan's home away from home when he's out farming and whitebaiting. Here a happy camper smartens himself up.

BELOW

Saltwater Creek below Fox Glacier, South Westland. Frigger's whitebaiting bach, despite its appearance, is a lovely weatherproof hideout in a southwesterly storm.
Rochelle Rafferty

Taverners in the Taramakau Valley, Westland.

Jacksons, Westland. Millers Flat is a twenty-acre patch of paradise on the true right of the Taramakau Valley.

Cecil King's historic slab hut, Wangapeka Track, Kahurangi National Park. Cecil King built this hut in the mid 1930s while prospecting for gold as part of a Government relief scheme.
Rochelle Rafferty

THIS PAGE AND RIGHT
Arthur's Pass. Two small
baches situated between
the Bealey River and
railway line to the West
Coast.
Rochelle Rafferty

Mrs Brown's cottage was built with stones from the nearby Bealey River in 1926. It enjoys an outstanding view across the Bealey Valley to the Devils Punchbowl waterfall.
Rochelle Rafferty

Main Road, Arthur's Pass. A portable bach, complete with potbelly stove, living quarters, work space and alfresco shower and hot tub.
Rochelle Rafferty

Charm personified at Arthur's Pass.
Jo Edgar

THIS PAGE
Originally built for the men who dug the Otira Tunnel in 1906, these are now charming holiday baches.
Rochelle Rafferty

LEFT
Paddy Freaney having a chinwag with Juliette Mowatt.

BOTTOM
The interior of a tunneller's cottage owned by Barney and Juliette Mowatt.
Rochelle Rafferty

Lochinvar, a three-hour journey from Arthur's Pass Road, was built by George Barns in the 1950s.
Rochelle Rafferty

Cauldur's bach at Lake Pearson, on Arthur's Pass Road. It was built by the current owner Maurice Cauldur's father in the days when you just asked a farmer if you could put a bach on his property.
Rochelle Rafferty

Roadman's Castle Hill. An original roadman's hut set among the limestone outcrops of Castle Hill Station.
Rochelle Rafferty

LEFT
Lake Alexandrina, west of Lake Tekapo, is an extremely beautiful and peaceful place. There are two main settlements of huts – the South End and the Outlet. This photo is of some of the huts and boathouses at the Outlet.
Geoff Cloake

THIS PAGE
Jan and John Gilbert purchased this hut at the Outlet in May 1978, and six months later were faced with extensive repairs after winds of over 100 knots virtually demolished it.
John Gilbert

LEFT

And why wouldn't you rebuild when you enjoy a view like this? Looking north over Lake Alexandrina to the Cass Gorge and the main divide of the Southern Alps.

Rose Grigor

BOTTOM

Some of the huts at the Outlet don't match the beautiful surroundings.

Jeff Grigor

LEFT
Situated on the banks of the stream joining Lake Alexandrina and Lake McGregor, this old rabbiter's hut has been named Smash Palace by its present owners.
Jeff Grigor

BOTTOM

Geoff Cloake

This hut was
owned by the
South Canterbury
RSA. Situated
at the Outlet it
has very recently
sold for around
$250,000.

*South Canterbury
RSA*

Two further huts at the Outlet, Lake Alexandrina.
John Gilbert

The settlement of the southern end of Lake Alexandrina has no electricity and access is by a private road.

Nobody I spoke to could remember seeing anyone staying at this hut at the southern end of Lake Alexandrina.
Jeff Grigor

SOUTH ISLAND

This photograph was taken around 1948 when the owner of the hut, Cecil Davies, shifted it from Timaru. At that time it was one of the very few huts at the southern end of Lake Alexandrina.

Photo supplied by Alan Bower

ABOVE
When the weather permits, much of the cooking is done on the barbecue outside.
Russell Potts

RIGHT
The hut has been enlarged since then but it is still very compact. Alan Bower, one of the current owners, sits inside enjoying a quiet moment.

THIS PAGE AND RIGHT
This hut in the Southern Alps is situated at an altitude of 5025 feet. Sometimes in winter you have to dig your way in.
Roland Dale

TOP RIGHT
The harsh climate means maintenance is a priority every summer.

RIGHT
Nevis Jones and Grant Keeley jamming at 5025 feet on what is one of the highest pianos in New Zealand.

FAR RIGHT
The view from the toilet makes it difficult to concentrate on what you are in there to do.
Roland Dale

TOP
Lake Coleridge.
Yes, the wheels
are off, so
it definitely
qualifies as a
bach!

BOTTOM
First you remove
the caravans'
wheels, and then
you build a roof
between them.
Next, a door is
added and the
room enclosed.
Lake Coleridge.

RIGHT
The final stage – front
door and windows.
Geoff Cloake

ABOVE

There are very few huts away from the village on Lake Tekapo, but this one was built by Russell Hervey at the site known as the Cherry Orchard in the 1950s. His son is the current owner.

Mark Hervey

LEFT

This houseboat is moored at Sailors Cutting on the Ahuriri Arm of Lake Benmore.

Geoff Cloake

RIGHT

Hobson Bay, north of Taylors Mistake, Banks Peninsula. In the 1890s the first baches appeared, many as walled off caves.

Elizabeth Jarman

SOUTH ISLAND

Hobson Bay.
Elizabeth Jarman

Further to the south is Boulder Bay. Originally access was only by boat or a track around the hills. Since World War Two it has been possible to drive around to Godley Head, directly above Boulder Bay, and then walk down some 950 feet of track to access the bay.
Geoff Cloake

Boulder Bay is home to a colony of little blue penguins who nest under the baches. The pale yellow bach is a converted army prefab, one of many such huts readily available in 1946.

Norman Webb

These two Boulder Bay baches were built of local boulders mortared together and were the original buildings in the bay.

Norman Webb

LEFT
Ataahua South, at the southern end of Banks Peninsula.

BOTTOM
A converted railway carriage north of Kaikoura.
Mark Brimblecombe

Birdlings Flat is between
Lake Ellesmere and the
sea at the southern end
of Banks Peninsula.
Fishing is the main
occupation here.
Stephanie Dore

The north side of the Rakaia River mouth. The rivers of the Canterbury Plains are renowned especially for their salmon fishing. As a consequence, there are settlements of baches at the mouths of all its rivers.
Jo Edgar

BACHES & CRIBS

North side of the Rakaia
River mouth.
Jo Edgar

RIGHT
There is a substantial settlement of baches on the south side of the Rakaia River mouth.

BOTTOM
An early split-level bach?
Jo Edgar

RIGHT
Rakaia South.
Jo Edgar

RIGHT
Hakatere is the
settlement at the mouth
of the Ashburton River.
Jo Edgar

BACHES & CRIBS

LEFT
Hakatere. It is always a good idea to ensure your colour scheme blends with the local surroundings.
Jo Edgar

Hakatere.
Is the cat a
permanent
resident? The
butterfly is going
nowhere fast.
Jo Edgar

LEFT AND RIGHT
Because the Rangitata
River mouth is in
South Canterbury the
residences are referred
to as 'huts'.
Jo Edgar

The big sky of the Canterbury Plains. Rangitata River mouth.
Jo Edgar

Twenty kilometres inland from the Opihi River mouth is the township of Pleasant Point. Less than a kilometre out of town on the banks of the Opihi a settlement of huts has been established.
Jo Edgar

LEFT AND RIGHT
Pleasant Point.

BOTTOM
On the north bank of the Opihi river mouth is the settlement of Milford. Whitebaiting, salmon and trout fishing are popular here.
Jo Edgar

Two kilometres inland from the mouth of the Opihi River on the south side are the Waipopo huts. I spent most of my childhood holidays here.
Jeff Grigor

The Moeraki Peninsula situated south of Oamaru has become famous for its boulders and for the café, Fleurs Place. Moeraki has great fishing, abundant wildlife and an eclectic mixture of cribs. This crib is situated at Katiki Point on the southeast corner of the peninsula, near the lighthouse.

Jo Edgar

These cribs sit in the township of Moeraki, and overlook the harbour.
Jo Edgar

RIGHT

Looking across from Tikoraki Point to the wonderful small bay called the Kaik.

John McGlashan

BELOW

The Kaik, on the eastern side of the Moeraki Peninsula, is home to seals, penguins and a wonderful collection of cribs.

Jeff Grigor

I was informed by a local that Keri Hulme wrote *The Bone People* while living in this crib, and that Ralph Hotere owns a crib in the settlement.
Jeff Grigor

More Kaik cribs in need of a little care and attention.

ABOVE
Jeff Grigor

LEFT
Rose Grigor

The Kaik. A beautiful
view of the bay from
this crib.
Jo Edgar

BACHES & CRIBS

A high tide washes up
against the cribs at the
Kaik.
Jeff Grigor

Shag Point is a few
kilometres south
of Moeraki and is a
charming settlement.
This crib with an
outstanding view is
called Paua Cottage.
John McGlashan

LEFT
Further out on
the peninsula is
this crib with its
beautiful garden.
Rose Grigor

SOUTH ISLAND

123

RIGHT
Comfort at Shag Point.
John McGlashan

BOTTOM
Only the TV aerial lets on that this Shag Point crib is still being used.
Jeff Grigor

A classic New Zealand crib with a wonderful view, Shag Point.
Jeff Grigor

Situated in the Cardrona Valley between Wanaka and Queenstown.
Stephanie Dore

RIGHT
This dry stone cottage was built by a gold prospector in the nineteenth century. It sits in the Wharehuanui Valley under the slopes of Coronet Peak.
Jeff Grigor

ABOVE
Cribs of this age require constant maintenance.

LEFT
Enjoying a strong gin and a spectacular view.
Lee Keeley

One of three historic gold miners' cottages in Arrowtown, which is now used as a holiday crib. I rented this cottage when I lived in Arrowtown in the early 1970s.
Rosemary Smart

Purakaunui is a beautiful inlet on the north side of the Otago Peninsula. This crib was built in the 1870s by members of the local iwi, who made a living supplying fish to whalers in the area. Maude Nisbet, a Shakespearean enthusiast, bought the crib in 1910 and named it As You Like It.
Nevis Jones

This Purakaunui crib was built in the 1880s by Dunedin builder George Lawrence for his daughter Emily. It was purchased in 1950 by Maude Nisbet's daughter and son-in-law, and then in 1970 by their son. It enjoys a magnificent view down the estuary towards Goat Island.

Nevis Jones

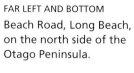

FAR LEFT AND BOTTOM
Beach Road, Long Beach, on the north side of the Otago Peninsula.

LEFT
Karitane is an old fishing village about fifty kilometres north of Dunedin.
John Barton

On the road between
Dunedin and Aramoana,
Otago Peninsula.
Joan Titchener.

THIS PAGE AND RIGHT
A very popular holiday spot at the mouth of the Taieri
River, not far south of Dunedin.
Mark Brimblecombe

Toko Mouth, a
settlement at the mouth
of the Tokomariro River,
east of Milton, South
Otago.
Mark Brimblecombe

ABOVE AND TOP RIGHT
Toko Mouth.
Mark Brimblecombe

RIGHT
Toko Mouth. Yes, it is still habitable.
John Barton

Thistle Do at Measly
Beach, southeast of
Milton, South Otago.

Measly Beach, South
Otago. Part of Wairoa
appears to be an old
railway carriage.
Mark Brimblecombe

ABOVE
The old Chaslands School now converted into a holiday crib complete with tennis court.
John Barton

RIGHT
The sign above the door says Chaslands 1897 and this crib is situated at Chaslands in The Catlins.
Mark Brimblecombe

Another remote Fiordland crib, this time in the Lower Hollyford Valley, east of Milford Sound.

Ian Grigor

Is this the most isolated crib in New Zealand? Situated in Fiordland somewhere between Dusky Sound and Chalky Inlet. It is built entirely of flotsam scavenged off the beaches.
Roland Dale